The Pi

Seven Lessons to Help Pilots Land
Safely in Retirement

"The Pilot's Advisor"

Ryan J. Fleming

MBA, RICP, CRPC

PREFACE

This retirement guide is being written by a Pilot (me) specifically for Pilots (all of you). This is my best attempt to translate and put into "pilot speak" many of the pitfalls and dangers that you face in planning for a safe landing in retirement.

I have been learning from the best financial advisors in the industry since 2008, none more impressive than Dan Cuprill. I am writing this book with the help of this mentor and many of the ideas in this book come from the seminars he has given throughout his career and our pointed discussions and analysis together. Dan has been conducting retirement planning seminars for over twenty years! (Yeah, he is pretty old). Planning for retirement can be stressful and mistakes in this planning can have drastic affects. I like to think about it in flying terms. There are many emergencies in an airplane that can be resolved and aren't that big of a deal as long as we run the right checklists, stick to the plan, and of course, assuming we have enough fuel. However, if we fail to plan, and don't divert, we tragically won't reach out destination safely.

I'll admit up front that I am sometimes guilty of not always being politically correct and sometimes say things that my wife explains to me as being "inappropriate." So, for this, I will apologize in advance. I'm a crew dog and even worse, a cargo pilot. (FedEx and C-17s in the Air Force)

However, I want this book to be different. This is a book that is unlike any other personal finance book. My goal for this book is to be a book about personal finance and planning that has very few numbers.

I know there is enough books about investing and finance that have plenty of numbers, and I also know I am not smart enough to improve on them! This book is also short, and that is by design. One, because I am lazy, and two, because it is written for Pilots! (I can say this because I am one!)

In this book, we will describe and analyze many of the quantitative aspects of personal finance, but like most aircraft accidents, human behavior is to blame. The biggest obstacle to investor success is the investor's OWN mistakes. We are only human, and as humans, we naturally want to avoid pain. We seek pleasure when we can, but the absence of pain is paramount.

This "survival mechanism" kept early cavemen motivated to stay warm, to find food, and to avoid saber tooth tigers. Today, it keeps us fat, avoiding exercise (which for many is painful), and eating fast food and ice cream (which is pleasurable).

In today's society, this "survival mechanism" and affinity for "instant gratification" has also caused the average investor, according to the DALBAR Quantitative Analysis of Investor Behavior, to buy high (because winners bring pleasure and we want more of that) and to sell low (so we can avoid even more pain).

This emotional behavior by the average investor results in sub-par rates of return. The survival instinct that saved the caveman and allowed him to evolve is the same instinct that destroys the average investor's portfolio.

As pilots, we don't like turbulence, but that doesn't mean we should ignore that it is out there or fly so low that we run out of fuel. We need to have a plan and make unemotional decisions based on aviation experience and not "get-home-itis".

As investors, at the beginning, we accept the premise that returns will not be consistent and that there is inherent risk; but we totally forget it as soon as we suffer a down month, or God forbid, a down year. Rather than logically accept that returns, like life, are never linear, we panic, convincing ourselves that this time the apocalypse is real. Then, we emotionally sell or make some other emotional decision that hurts our portfolio.

Of course, once the zombies fail to appear at our doorstep in search of flesh, we then realize the error of our ways and start investing again...after the market has already recovered and we already cut off our own head, missing out on the recovery.

In addition to fighting the natural survivor tendencies of our brain, we are constantly inundated with the talking heads on Fox Business and CNBC. Or, what about Money Magazine and Kiplinger's?

All of these entities don't care about the actual market and how it works! They are in the business of selling ratings and magazines!

They realize they can sell more if they induce fear and promote greed. We need to see past this "financial porn" (I told you I wasn't always politically correct) and not fall victim to the fear! Turn off the talking heads and focus on prudent academic investing principles. Get rid of the emotion.

Another major threat that the average investor must be rescued from is taxation. Unlike past generations, Baby Boomers and beyond must deal with the intricacies of having their retirement savings tied up in accounts like 401K's, 403B's, and IRA's. We are now completely responsible for planning for our own retirements. Pensions are a thing of the past and are almost totally extinct.

Almost all of these accounts have never been taxed and Uncle Sam is smart. He will get his money. We are happy that the taxes have been "deferred" but ultimately, Uncle Sam is patiently waiting to tax you on the bigger portion that this account has grown to over time. You are business partners and Uncle Sam still hasn't taken his cut. If you think all that money in your 401K is yours, you couldn't be more wrong!

Uncle Sam will get paid eventually and with the ever-growing national debt and the looming social security crisis, do you think there is any chance that taxes might go up? The money is going to come from somewhere and I have a pretty good idea of who is going to be responsible for bringing money to the table.

And lastly, speaking of social security... When should I take it? Will it still be there? How is the government going to finance it? Will it be taxed? Will the tax on it continue to increase? And what about long term healthcare? Medicaid and Medicare? Many questions and no solid answers. Think this can add to the emotion when dealing with your finances?

So, now with all the responsibility, is the individual investor simply doomed to fail? I don't think so. However, without getting help or understanding the challenges that you will be facing is like flying straight into a storm while having your radar turned off! You must turn on the radar and start understanding what is ahead of you, so that you might turn the odds in your favor. I urge you to come fly with and let's explore these issues. So, let's take off, together, put the gear up, and start to navigate around this storm together!

– Ryan J. Fleming, MBA, RICP, CRPC

"The Pilot's Advisor"

Want to make $8 million dollars more over the course of your career in saving for retirement? Then, I urge you to watch this short 10 minute webinar that could save you retirement.

www.pilotsadvisor.com

CONTENTS

Lesson One: "No One Can Predict the Future,

So Please Stop Trying!"...1

Lesson Two: Mr. Parker knew what he was talking about!...........11

Lesson Three: Your Biggest Fears will come True! 17

Lesson Four: It will End Badly!...24

Lesson Five: We Are Our Own Worst Enemy! 28

Lesson Six: Social Security and the Modern Day Ponzi Scheme ..37

Lesson Seven: To get Flat Abs or To Earn True Wealth

Requires a Coach!..42

My Offer to You 50

Appendices...53

APPENDIX I...54

Appendix II 61

Appendix III...74

Appendix IV...83

Appendix V 89

Appendix VI...98

About the Author 106

"NO ONE CAN PREDICT THE FUTURE, SO PLEASE STOP TRYING!"

"Uncertainty is the only certainty there is, and knowing how to live with insecurity is the only security."

-- John Allen Paulos

Imagine a TV network dedicated to fortune telling. Every day, this network would have highly educated people who strongly believe they can predict the future. One after the other, they come onto the network and tell their predictions for free. They talk about the impending crashes and how life as we know it will cease to exist. What if they were wrong 80% of the time? Would you keep watching? Would you find value in the words that are coming out of their mouths? Despite these failures, we as a society continue to watch.

Even worse, many stake their entire fortunes and retirement plans on the advice of these people. Would you continue to watch?

Millions do. What we have just described here is the "financial porn" of Fox Business and CNBC.

I know you can't help yourself. Turn it on. Just like we can't help ourselves from watching "Top Gun" all over again anytime it pops up on the TV screen.

So, turn it on around noon in the middle of the week. Chances are, some "expert" will be giving you his free stock tips or some insight into where the market is heading. He knows, but no one else does. Just wait, there will be another "expert" right after him. He'll tell you the future for free. Did we mention they are wrong over 80% of the time?

Here is a little reality: No one, and I mean no one, knows where investment markets are headed in the next week, month, or year. If they did know, they certainly wouldn't give that information away to you for free. In fact, they wouldn't tell you any information at all because it would be far too valuable to even sell.

Markets react to News.

Wouldn't you agree that markets react to news? Every time stocks drop in price, isn't there always some news event attributed to it (9/11, oil prices, the fed raising interest rates, China's currency)?

News is unpredictable.

Wouldn't you agree that news is unpredictable? Do you know about news events before they occur? Did you know any of these news events were going to happen?

1. Hijacked airplanes crashing into the World Trade Center and the Pentagon.
2. The Kennedy Assassination.
3. A Boeing 777 would simply vanish from the earth.
4. Arthur Anderson's false accounting of Enron.

In response to each of these news events, equity markets dropped rapidly. If you did know about these events a week before they actually occurred, you could have made billions of dollars. The talking heads all predicted that the market would crash if Donald J. Trump was elected President of the United States. Funny. The exact opposite happened and in a big way! Unfortunately, too many Americans missed out on this boom because they let the fear take over their decision making.

Two movies come to mind that demonstrate this reality.

Casino Royale (2006): James Bond seeks to defeat a card-playing terrorist who makes huge rates of return by shorting stocks on companies and then staging acts of sabotage on those corporations because he knows itwill drive down their stock price. In other words, he knows the news before anyone else because he's creating it.

Wall Street (1987): Gordon Gekko hires aspiring trader Bud Fox to "stop sending me information and start bringing me some." So, Bud breaks into offices at night, spies on company executives, and relays insider information told to him by his father. As a result, Gekko has "news" that no one else has, allowing him to trade ahead of the market.

So, if you agree that news is unpredictable and market performance reacts to news, can't we logically determine that markets are totally unpredictable?

Wait a minute. Are you saying that all those Wall Street experts like Jim Cramer really have no idea what they're talking about? Yes, pretty much.

Yes and no. They certainly know many things and are intelligent people. But so are millions of other traders. Everything everyone knows is already factored into a stock's price. It's what they don't know, the future news, which will drive stock prices. They are simply speculating as to what they think the news will be.

Sometimes they get it right, however, most of the time they get it wrong. Studies show that on average 80% of all professional portfolio managers fail to beat their benchmark index. Of the 20% that do, there are very few that can consistently do it over time.

The Law of Large Numbers

I am a huge Ohio State Buckeyes fan, so bear with me. Imagine that we filled the Horseshoe Stadium in Columbus, Ohio, with 35,000 people. (hardly filling that stadium that seats over 100,000). On the PA system, we instruct them all to stand up and remove a quarter from their pocket.

On our mark, they all flip the coin. Those who flipped heads (about 17,500) remain standing. Those who flipped tails sit down.

We now repeat the exercise, again and again. With 35,000 people flipping coins, we are willing to bet our houses that at least one person in the "Shoe" will flip heads ten times in a row. In fact, we wouldn't be surprised at all if at least 20 people did it.

The law of large numbers states that if you have enough people try to do something, someone will succeed regardless of their skill level. The individual who tossed heads 10 times in a row…is he or she an expert coin flipper? Does he or she somehow understand the gravitational properties between their quarter, wrist, and gravitational pull of the earth? Or were they just lucky?

Guess how many professional portfolio managers exist today? Yup, that's right, about 35,000! Over 2,000 work for Fidelity alone! Someone is bound to speculate correctly on the market's reaction to news that has yet to occur.

The successful coin flipper is called lucky. The successful stock picker is called a guru and gets his face on magazine covers.

Again, I will concede that most of these people are very smart. Most went to the very best business schools in the country where they were taught that markets and stock prices were not predictable. But, somewhere along the line, after they arrived on Wall Street, they were told how their firms really make money: trades. And despite its lack of academic merit, active management was reborn even though we know via numbers and statistics that it hurts the individual investor.

Over 1 billion trades a month at $9 per trade on the New York Stock Exchange alone. You do the math. It is in their best interest to trade…. but, not yours!

We do not think that these very smart people honestly believe they have found a peek into the future. If there were only a handful of them researching companies, then they might actually be onto something. But there are thousands, all crunching the same data.

Furthermore, their efforts to buy and sell ahead of the market incur the costs that ultimately lowers their rates of return.

In 2013, Eugene Fama won the Nobel Prize in economics for stating in the 1960's that something is worth only what someone is willing to pay for it. Called the Efficient Market Hypothesis, Fama showed (with a bunch of math) that the current price of the stock or bond is the correct price. Nothing is overvalued or undervalued until someone offers or agrees to a different price.

If you buy a house for $300,000, spend $50,000 for improvement, and put it up for sale, how much is it worth if the highest offer you receive is $290,000?

Correct. It's worth $290,000.

So, if it's true for real estate, why not stocks?

The $6 watch

Zach Norris is a young man with a passion for fine watches. Understanding that often people don't know the value of their old jewelry, he routinely visits thrift shops and garage sales looking for great deals. If he sees a watch that he knows he can quickly resell for a profit, he will buy it for the asking price and then quickly find a new buyer. In January of 2015, he bought a $6 watch at his local Goodwill store and then sold it for $35,000.

Norris is to watches what Wall Street portfolio managers aspire to be to stocks. But unlike Mr. Norris, they deal in public information. Had Goodwill known the watch was worth $35,000, would they have sold it for $6? Or, would the prior owner have given away the watch to Goodwill in the first place? Of course not. Mr. Norris had insider knowledge. In this case, he can legally act on it. But in the world of security trading, such a move will land you in jail (see Martha Stewart and Bud Fox).

Perhaps there was a time when news traveled slowly enough for someone to get a jump.

Those days are over.

No one can predict the future! News occurs randomly, and so too will stock and bond prices. All we have going for us is that over the history of mankind, good news has outperformed bad. Despite world wars, famines, epidemics, assassinations, national debt, and disco, capitalism finds a way to improve the quality of life. The quality of your life today dwarfs that of every king and queen of the Middle Ages. It dwarfs that of your great grandparents, and even your grandparents. Is it not only logical to assume that in the future we will witness massive amounts of bad news, but overall, we will prosper?

Optimistically is the realistic way to view the future. Hence, actions like market timing and stock picking are far less likely to succeed than buying, holding, and rebalancing a globally diversified portfolio.

Don't just take my word for it (books to read)

The Investment Answer by Daniel Goldie and Gordon Murray

Random Walk Down Wall Street by Burton Malkeil

The Smartest Investment Book You'll Ever Own by Dan Solin

What Wall Street Doesn't Want You to Know by Larry

Swedroe

<u>Winning the Loser's Game</u> by Charles Ellis

MR. PARKER KNEW WHAT HE WAS TALKING ABOUT!

"Mathematics are well and good, but human nature keeps dragging us around by the nose."

– Albert Einstein

You remember Mr. Parker...the figurehead math teacher from your high school who had been teaching there since the beginning of time. He had been teaching out of the same book because "the math hasn't changed." As you looked at the inside cover of the book, you saw the names and years of the prior holders. "Was it as boring for Tony Gentry in 1968 as it is for me now?" you asked yourself. "Was Mr. Parker cool back then?"

The one question that rose above all others was, "Will I ever need to know this stuff?"

Mr. Parker assured us we would. Now you're about to see that once again, he was right.

Meet Maverick and Iceman.

When not playing volleyball on the beach with their jeans on, they are drawing income from their savings accumulated from years of flying with their hair on fire, inverted, at Mach one for the United States Navy. Aside from any new horrible Tom Cruise movies that come out, they are pretty much retired.

Always living on the edge and being "dangerous", Maverick has invested heavily in equities under the belief that over time he stands to earn a higher rate of return.

Chances are he'll be right.

Iceman is no stranger to machismo, but opts for a portfolio that is likely to produce a lower, more consistent rate of return because like flying, he prefers to be Ice Cold and consistent, with no mistakes. Starting with one million each, they both desire to withdraw $50,000 per year to supplement their Navy retirement checks.

Maverick and Iceman are about to learn what Mr. Parker taught us years ago.

AVERAGE MAY NOT BE AS IMPORTANT AS CONSISTENCY OF RETURN.

Iceman: $1,000,000				Maverick: $1,000,000 Year			
Year	Withdrawal	Return	Y/E Value		Withdrawal	Return	Y/E Value
1	$50,000.00	6%	$1,007,000.00	1	$50,000.00	-13	$826,500.00
2	$50,000.00	8%	$1,087,560.00	2	$50,000.00	-20%	$661,200.00
3	$50,000.00	7%	$1,163,689.20	3	$50,000.00	5%	$694,260.00
4	$50,000.00	11%	$1,236,195.01	4	$50,000.00	-7%	$599,161.80
5	$50,000.00	-4%	$1,138,747.21	5	$50,000.00	20%	$658,994.16
6	$50,000.00	6%	$1,154,072.04	6	$50,000.00	25%	$761,242.70
7	$50,000.00	12%	$1,236,560.69	7	$50,000.00	-25%	$533,432.03
8	$50,000.00	-2%	$1,162,829.48	8	$50,000.00	45%	$700,976.44
9	$50,000.00	10%	$1,224,112.42	9	$50,000.00	30%	$846,269.37
10	$50,000.00	6%	**$1,244,559.17**	10	$50,000.00	20%	***$908,060.56***
Return Average: 6%				Return Average: 8%			

As you can see, although Maverick earned a higher average return (8% vs. 6%) at the end of ten years, he has considerably less money than his Top Gun wingman. Why? Every year, the two sell a part of their portfolios' shares to generate cash. When shares rise in value, it requires fewer shares to generate $50,000. When share prices fall, Maverick must sell more. Those extra shares, once sold, are gone. It matters not what his Portfolio does in the future in relation to those shares. He will never get them back By minimizing his potential downside, Iceman has more money even though he averaged less over time. Fewer negative years allows him to sell fewer shares.

This phenomenon exists only because Maverick and Iceman need to sell shares for cash. Had they never needed to sell shares, then Maverick would have more much money than Iceman, despite the volatility. This is the Math of Retirement.

Mr. Parker taught us that nothing in life performs consistently--not the weather, not your golf score, and certainly not an investment portfolio. This lack of consistency can be measured. It is called standard deviation. The lower the standard deviation, the more likely you will earn the average return each and every year. So, if you found a portfolio with a guaranteed return of 8% every year, then the standard deviation would be zero. Good luck finding that. Chances are, the best you'll do in seeking your 8% is a portfolio with a standard deviation of ten. So, what does that mean?

If Average Return is 8% and Standard Deviation is ten, then:
66% of the time: You will have a one year return between -2% and 18%.
95% of the time: You will have a one year return between -12% and 28%.
99% of the time: You will have a one year return between -22% and 38%.

If you are an investor, then your portfolio also has a long-term average return and a standard deviation to go along with it. The problem is that very few people understand this, nor do they understand the "normal" volatility that comes with it. If they did, we think they would be much less likely to panic.

For example, if a portfolio has the dimensions described in the chart above, should we be surprised (or even disappointed) if we earn a return of -6% in a given year?

Absolutely not. We already know going in that this is very likely. We also know that over time, it's more likely that we'll have more positive results than negative results. Guaranteed? No. Likely? Yes.

Think of it like flying an airplane across the country. The normal person would think that going in a straight line would be the quickest way to get there. Well, with the winds aloft and the shape of the earth, this is not the case.

Results do not come in a linear fashion, no matter how badly we wish they did. What in life does? Does your fantasy football QB get the same number of points each week? Do you always make the same number of free throws when you do best out of 10? Does it always take the same time to fly from Memphis to Savannah? Can you lift the same amount of weight in the gym every day? If any of these aren't the same, do you quit or have you learned to trust the process?

It is essential that you know the long-term average return and standard deviation of your portfolio allocation. Without knowing, you are simply winging it; and your survival mechanism stands a much better chance of over-riding your logic.

Know your math. Make Mr. Rex Parker proud!

Don't just take my word for it (books to read):

The Intelligent Asset Allocator by William Bernstein

All About Asset Allocation by Richard Feri

Asset Allocation by Roger Gibson

YOUR BIGGEST FEARS WILL COME TRUE!

"The only two things that scare me are God and the IRS"

– Dr. Dre

Assuming that you do not define patriotism by the amount you pay in tax, what follows should be useful.

If you're one of the 53% of Americans who pay federal income taxes, then it is likely you pay more than what is legally required. If you own a small business or are a commercial airline pilot, then I can almost guarantee that you are over paying!

The Seven Most Expensive Words in the English Language: My CPA takes care of my taxes.

From myexperience, most CPAs do a great job of filing taxes; but very few actually do any real tax planning.

When I ask people, when was the last time their CPA said he found a way to lower your taxes by $4,000, they usually give me a blank stare and then say, "Never."

Does your CPA/Tax Preparer ever:

- Call you with proactive strategies to achieve a tax-free retirement?
- Demonstrate how to restructure your 401k/403b/IRA accounts to avoid future taxation?
- Teach you how to collect your social security benefits TAX FREE?
- Show you how to structure your business to minimize employment taxes?
- Show you how to write off your family's medical bills as a business expense?

- Show you how you can hire children (or grandchildren) to shift income from yourself to them?

- Explain how each of your investments is taxed and make suggestions on how to reduce it?

- Advise you on how to carefully consider which investments belong in taxable accounts and which investments belong in tax-advantaged accounts?

- Develop a plan for maximizing the value of any long-term capital loss carrying forward?

- Explain the rules governing "passive" income and losses and have a plan to avoid "suspended" losses?

- Meet with you throughout the year to discuss your business--or does he just wait until taxes are due?

- Give you a plan for minimizing taxes--or does he/she just wing it every year?

Aside from investing behavior, income taxes are the greatest obstacle to most investors. There is never an age at which you stop paying them. You paid tax on your social security as you put the money into the system, and you will likely pay tax on the money as it comes out.

When you reach age 70.5, you must start paying tax on your retirement plans (401k, IRA, 403b). When you die, your heirs must also pay tax on whatever is left!

Your estate may be taxed again for simply being too big!

The code is, by design, very complicated. Too often, people just go along with it, unaware of the steps that can legally reduce their federal and state income taxes. This is even more important when planning for retirement.

You have a choice of paying taxes now...or later. To many, procrastination seems logical when it comes paying the IRS. For years people have socked away massive amounts of money in 401ks, 403bs, and IRAs.

The idea is you invest it now in a tax- deductible account while you're in a high tax bracket. Then you withdraw it at a lower tax bracket when you retire. Or so you hope.

What if taxes rise in the future? Our country, as of 2016, owes close to $20 trillion. Projections suggest this amount will continue to rise as more and more baby boomers retire. Fewer people are paying taxes and more requiring things like Medicare, Medicaid, and Social Security.

Case Study

Bill & Karen Tucker are both 65. Retired, they each have a rollover IRA worth $600,000. Bill collects $2,200 a month from social security.

Karen receives $1,800. They need $7,000 a month to live comfortably, so they withdraw $3,000 a month from their retirement accounts.

To determine how much of their social security check is subject to taxation, we add the IRA withdrawals ($36,000) to one-half of the social security payments ($24,000).

This gives them a modified adjusted gross income (MAGI) of $60,000. Whenever the MAGI exceeds $44,000 for a married couple, then up to 85% of their check is subjected to taxation.

Assuming they file jointly and use the standard deduction, Bill & Karen owe $4,300 in Federal income taxes. However, what if they had decided a few years back to convert their IRAs to a

Roth IRA? Doing so would have triggered taxes at the time of conversion, but no tax would ever be owned on the accounts ever again. Even if their accounts doubled in value, there is no tax associated with a Roth withdrawal.

Not only is there no tax on Roth IRA withdrawals, but now there would also be no tax owed on their Social Security benefits. Furthermore, Bill & Karen could now withdraw an additional $16,400 from their taxable IRA and still pay $0 in tax since they still have their standard deduction and exemption to apply.

Imagine if federal income tax rates double in the future. By converting to a Roth, the Tucker's have protected their retirement assets.

Another tax-advantaged vehicle is permanent life insurance. Money in the policy grows tax deferred and can be accessed tax free via a policy loan. While I don't usually recommend retirees buy life insurance, this feature is a great reason to keep your policy even after you've stopped working.

Like most of the prospects we meet, the Tuckers rely solely on their accountant for tax advice. But from our experience, many accountants work as tax filers, not strategic tax planners.

Tax planning is one of the most ignored areas of financial planning, and the failure to address IRS lien on savings is ruining people. It is not the job of the IRS to tell you how to lower your taxes. It's your job. If you don't know how, you need to find a professional who does. You won't find him inside a box of turbo tax software.

The tax code is very complicated. Too often people just go along with it, unaware of the steps that can legally reduce their federal and state income taxes. Failure to address this issue early can mean you're not worth anywhere close to what you think.

If you want to know more about real tax planning, call us at 843-475-3038. We'll show you how we use our Tax Blueprint™ to rescue retirement assets for our clients.

Don't just take our word for it (books to read):

How to Pay Zero Taxes 2016 by J.K. Lasser

The Power of Zero by David McKnight

IT WILL END BADLY!

"It's paradoxical, that the idea of living a long life appeals to everyone, but the idea of getting old doesn't appeal to anyone."

– Andy Rooney

The first chapter ended with a statement that the future is always likely to be better than the past. For society as a whole, we truly believe that. As for our individual lives, we know that life is finite. The Grim Reaper is undefeated. And while modern medicine has made huge strides in fighting heart disease, diabetes, and cancer, we all still all eventually die.

The lucky ones will die suddenly, or die doing something they love. Here today living life to the fullest…gone tomorrow. Sad for our loved ones, but much better than dying a slow death where our health declines daily, limited to a wheelchair, incapable of recalling our children's names, and needing assistance to visit the bathroom.

Depressing...isn't it? But, that's life.

As a society, we are living longer. That is a good thing, but that also means our money must last much longer. It means that eventually we will become weak and likely to need help with those things we only want to do for ourselves (custodial care).

Some stats from the National Institute for Health:

- If you reach age 65, there's a 70% chance you'll need custodial care.
- The average nursing home stay is almost three years.
- The average nursing home cost is
- $70,000 a year.
- Nursing home costs rise at twice the average inflation rate.
- Medicare doesn't pay for Long Term Care.
- Medicaid is available only after you've spent down your assets.

- Most people in nursing homes are on
- Medicaid, but they didn't start there.

Basically, you have three options when it comes to long-term care.

- First, you can self-insure the exposure. Perhaps you have enough money to do just that. Remember…it's $70,000 a year now. At 6% inflation, the price will double in twelve years. If you're married and you get sick, will that leave enough money for your healthy spouse?

- Second, you can rely on Medicaid. Why not? Most do, but, that's available only after you've spent down your own money. If you're married, Medicaid kicks in when you have about $100,000 left. You don't have to sell your house, but the government may attach a lien to it after you die so that it can recoup the cost of your care.

- Third, you can buy long-term care insurance. For many people, this is the right choice. Often we hear people say they won't buy it out of fear that they'll never use it, and thus waste their money. We're going to let you in on a little secret: the people who go to nursing homes with long term care don't win the game. It's those who have long-term care insurance but die peacefully in their sleep, healthy today...dead tomorrow, who win the game.

When your car isn't stolen, do you regret owning auto insurance? You should never regret making the prudent financial decision.

Long-term care insurance can be expensive, but a few things can be done to reduce it:

1. Limit coverage to four years. Odds are very high you won't need the policy after four years. By limiting coverage to four years, you reduce the cost dramatically over a lifetime benefit policy.

2. Self-insure a part of the cost. If nursing homes in your area cost $200 per day, consider coverage for $150. Be sure to study the long-term impact of not being fully insured.

3. Ask your children to pay for it. They are the ones who stand to benefit from you not spending all of their inheritance on nursing home care.

Whatever you do...have a plan! It's not a matter of if, but when!

Don't just take our word for it:

Long Term Care: <u>Your Financial Planning Guide</u> by Phyllis Shelton

WE ARE OUR OWN WORST ENEMY!

"We have seen the enemy, and he is us."

— Pogo

Perhaps the biggest obstacle (no, not *perhaps*...it really *is* the biggest) toward financial success is our own brain...our humanness...our emotions.

God gave us many gifts; but if misused, they can be very self-destructive.

Consider weight loss. Technically, losing weight is very easy. We simply exercise more and eat less. Yet, we are the fattest nation on earth; and weight loss is a multi-billion-dollar industry. Why?

Investing is also quite simple: buy when prices are low. Sell when they are high. According to the Dalbar study, we see that simple strategy ignored all the time. People often do the complete opposite.

Let's take Marty McFly's time traveling Delorean back a few years….to 10,000 BC. Meet your great, great, great, great, great, great, great, great, great (you get the idea) grandfather. We'll call him Fred. He lives in a cave with his mate Wilma and their children Pebbles and Bam Bam (whom they adopted after a T-Rex ate Barney and Betty Rubble).

Life is very simple for Fred and Wilma. Fred wakes up, sharpens his spear, and kills whatever he can find. He brings it back to the cave where Wilma cooks it.

Fred is motivated to stop the pains of hunger, cold, and predators. He seeks warmth and comfort where he can; but above all else, he tries to avoid pain for his family and himself. He doesn't know it, but Fred has within his brain a survival mechanism that motivates him to behave this way. It is his natural tendency to flee from danger. In fact, all animals have it--another gift from God. Fred doesn't worry about his cholesterol level, his A1C results, or his blood pressure. He merely wants to stay fed, stay warm, and stay safe. Fred was the original couch potato whenever the opportunity presented itself.

Food, water, safety, and warmth…that's all he thinks about. Morality, personal fulfillment, spirituality…. these do not matter to him at all. It's a struggle just to meet the basics.

Fast forward to present day. We don't have Fred's worries. We are far from those days. Food? In the US, a major health problem amongst our poor is obesity. Water and warmth…readily available.

The survival mechanism that kept Fred alive before a sabretooth tiger ate him is still present in our brains. We don't use it often, but it is there…lurking.

Need to lose weight by eating less (painful) and exercising (even more painful). Forget it. Our brain tells us we're crazy. Stay in bed.

Rest. Relax. I'll do it later. Tomorrow.

Fred didn't care if he lived past age 40, but you do. Rather than helping you though, the survival mechanism is betraying you.

When your stocks fall in value, you experience pain. Your brain tells you that you must do something. You must sell. You know you shouldn't sell when things are low, but you make an emotional decision and sell.

When what you sold starts increasing in value, you feel worse! You know logically that stocks are likely to rebound, but your brain convinces you that "this time it is different."

While the survival mechanism is the worst feature of our psyche when it comes to investing, there are a few others that can be equally destructive:

Herding.

When we were teenagers, we called it "peer pressure". Our mothers asked, "If Johnny told you to jump off a bridge, would you?" Hey, bridge jumping can be great fun.

When a pilot on the line tells you that everyone is dumping the index fund in the company 401k or buying this new biotech stock, and everyone is making tons of money off of it, you need to remind yourself of something. Unless said pilot is having secret meetings with the company chairman, he knows nothing more than the rest of the world. All the information about this company is already factored into the price of that stock.

These pilots are just speculating and gambling with their money. Sadly, there are several "pilots" who always know the latest hot stock or know that the banks are going to fail and we need to buy gold…and guns!

Confirmation Bias.

We'd all like to believe that we are objective thinkers, weighing all the facts before making a decision or establishing a belief. Sorry…but this is not true. Unfortunately, most of us are simply too lazy to do our own research.

There are things we WANT to believe are true. So much so, we'll ignore any evidence to the contrary.

Take my daughter, Jaden. At age 7, she is committed to believing in Santa Clause. She's heard from classmates that St.

Nick isn't real, but every year she finds evidence to the contrary (thanks to her mom). In her mind, the kids who don't believe are simply the ones who misbehave and receive nothing on December 25th.

For other people, we see confirmation bias in areas like climate change, the Kennedy assassination, or the future price of gold.

In 2008, I tried to talk my step dad Paul, who was a GE maintenance guy, out of having all of his portfolio in GE stock. He told me he had no intention of ever diversifying away from his company stock. "I don't want to hear it," he said to me when I suggested a globally diversified portfolio. Modern portfolio theory, I told him. He was 61, and the stock comprised 100% of his portfolio. In the previous ten years, his net worth had tripled.

It seemed invincible and he was very loyal to the company that had employed him over the past 30+ years.

At that point, the stock was trading at $65 a share. A few years later, it was worth $8 and today around $30.

When it comes to matters of finance, confirmation bias can be expensive and it can really hurt emotionally. I am proud to say that, today, Paul is letting me manage his portfolio!! The pain he felt was too great.

Gambler's Fallacy.

The roulette wheel has come up red the last six times. It must turn up black this time, right? No wait…six times in a row!! It has to turn up red a seventh time. It's on a roll. This fallacy reminds me of one of the best pilots I have flown with named Charley Mack.

He loved living on the edge in all forms of life and he especially loved gambling. I feel like I have heard this comment a hundred times, "put it on black, it has to be black!"

The Gambler believes that despite randomness, past events influence future events. This is why casinos give free hotel rooms to high rollers and people that continue to gamble. The casino knows the numbers. Just don't leave our casino!

We know eventually you will give the money back. You'll believe you have skill, but we know it is pure chance…and the odds of chance always favor the house. Always.

I also flew with a pilot we'll call "the Doctor." He at least had it right. He only played Blackjack because he knew that was the game that gave him the best odds. Despite what anyone said, "the Doctor" was unemotional at all times. He always did what the book told him to do. He knew it was just a game of odds. As he took another card that we knew would bust him, he always said, "unemotional, you got to be unemotional. It is what it is…"

We see it with stocks all the time. The market is up, and "experts" call for a "correction". In order for a correction to happen, we must first have a mistake. The "correction assumption" is that stocks are mispriced.

Eventually the market will wake up this reality, causing prices to adjust. It's hogwash. News drives stock prices. Markets will move randomly because news occurs randomly.

Anchoring.

Back to my step-dad Paul, the GE employee. My mom saw the potential mistake of holding just one stock, but even she couldn't be swayed toward logic because they knew diversification would trigger taxation and she knew Paul's passion for his GE stock. So anchored were they in their belief that they watched that GE stock ride itself all the way back down.

A successful investor understands that logic doesn't come naturally. He seeks out ways to ensure that when it comes to money, the left side of his brain stays in control. Like "the Doctor" said, you have to be "unemotional."

This right here is a huge reason for having the help of a financial coach who will help you stay on track and not make emotional decisions right at the point where it will hurt you the most.

Don't just take our word for it (books to read):
Predictably Irrational by Dan Ariely
The Behavior Gap by Carl Richards

SOCIAL SECURITY AND THE MODERN DAY PONZI SCHEME

"The real sin with Social Security is that it's a long-term rip-off and a short-term scam."

— Tony Snow

A Ponzi scheme is an investment fraud that involves the payment of purported returns to existing investors from funds contributed by new investors. Ponzi scheme organizers often solicit new investors by promising to invest funds in opportunities claimed to generate high returns with little or no risk. In many Ponzi schemes, the fraudsters focus on attracting new money to make promised payments to earlier- stage investors to create the false appearance that investors are profiting from a legitimate business.

With little or no legitimate earnings, Ponzi schemes require a consistent flow of money from new investors to continue. Ponzi schemes tend to collapse when it becomes difficult to recruit new investors or when a large number of investors ask to cash out.

United States Securities & Exchange Commission In the 2012 election primary, pundits attacked Texas Governor Rick Perry for correctly describing the Social Security system as a Ponzi scheme. The system, which began in 1937, then taxed 37 workers for every retiree a maximum total of $30 per year.

Today, it taxes three workers for every retiree 6.2% of their earnings (up to $118,550). If you're self-employed, you pay the tax twice.

Money is taken from workers and is transferred to retirees. The rate of return is not guaranteed. Most people will average between two and four percent. Many will lose money if they die before they receive benefits equal to their contributions. Unlike your savings, you cannot leave your social security benefits to your children. At least Charles Ponzi gave SOME investors a high rate of return.

Social Security today is not what it was intended to be when President Roosevelt signed the program into existence in 1935. Its original intent was to aid Americans who couldn't take care of themselves, such as widows and orphans. It was never designed to be the sole means for retirement income, which it has become for many Americans today.

In 1935, life expectancy was 58 years old. Even back then, the earliest one could collect benefits was age 65! On average, you were more likely to die than receive benefits. Ironically, the very first person to receive a check, Ida May Fuller, lived to be 100 years old. These days about 58 million people receive benefits.

Today, we have 10,000 baby boomers retiring every single day and starting to take benefits. Where is that money going to come from?

Benefit Timing

For many retirees, the question of when to take benefits can be a difficult one. The longer you wait to start collecting, the larger your monthly check. Full retirement age is between 62 and 67 depending on what year you were born.

You can take benefits as early as 62, but receive 25% less per month than if you hold out until your full retirement age. If you wait until age 70 to collect, then you get 32% more.

In real dollars that means if your full retirement benefit is $2,000 but you elected to take it at 62, you will receive $1,500 every month. Likewise, if you wait until age 70, you will receive $2,700 every month.

Life expectancy plays a major role in determining the timing of your social security benefits. The breakeven point for taking benefits at 62 vs. 70 is age 78.

If you had that time machine and knew your expiration date – no problem. Of course, if you delay taking your benefit, it may mean you have to spend more of your savings in the early years of retirement.

Many factors need to be taken into consideration when taking social security. For a free Social Security timing report, visit my mentor's, Dan Cuprill's website link at https://planfacts.com/dancuprill/ssgen#/ or you can go directly to his site at www.matsonandcuprill.com.

So what is the future of Social Security? Is it sustainable? What was once a 1% tax is now 6.2%. As fewer people pay in and more are recipients, the percentage could always be increased. The amount of income subject to the tax could be increased, and inflationary increases could be eliminated or decreased. Lots of appealing options...

No political party wants to broach the elimination of Social Security, and they likely won't. Social Security in its current state isn't at all what Roosevelt had in mind in 1935, so change is always a strong possibility.

Don't Just Take Our Word For It:
Get What's Yours: The Secrets to Maxing Out Your Social Security by Laurence J. Kotlikoff, Phillip Moeller and Paul Solman

---

TO GET FLAT ABS OR TO EARN TRUE WEALTH REQUIRES A COACH!

"Everyone needs a coach. It doesn't matter whether you're a basketball player, a tennis player, a gymnast or a bridge player."

-- Bill Gates

At age 51, he finally got the news: "Dan, you are fat, your blood sugar is too high, and so is your blood pressure. Other than that, you're doing great…for a 70-year-old."

He couldn't argue with the doctor. Everything he said was true.

"If you're serious about this, I can coach you through it," the doctor said. "Every three months, going forward, you will come in for new blood work and a review of your eating habits for the past three months. In addition, you will spend time with my personal nutritionist. Lastly, you will hire a personal trainer who will give you a full body workout three times a week." I remember Dan telling me this story and since we always talked about how simple the formula was for losing weight, we had some laughs.

Three months later, Dan had lost 15 pounds, and his blood sugar level (A1C) dropped from 7.1 to 5.7 (you want it below 6.5).

Could he have done it without the nutritionist and trainer? Technically, yes. Realistically, not a chance in hell. When the alarm goes off at 5:30 a.m., he now jumps out of bed because he knows the trainer is waiting for him at the gym. If it were up to Dan to work out alone, that alarm would never be set. He admits he would just procrastinate. When he did get around to exercising, it would be with half the intensity his trainer demands. Why?

Because exercise is painful and getting up early is painful! Sleep is pleasurable. Steel cut oatmeal doesn't taste nearly as good as Dunkin' Donuts or gravy poured all over your egg and potato mixture with bacon throughout! I call this the Dozier or the Garbage Plate!

On our own, we rarely perform at our optimal levels. A good coach will not only help you achieve excellence, he'll assist in keeping you there. A good coach sees things you can't (or at least don't want to see). He forces you to leave your comfort zone and to apply logic when emotion is in overdrive. He holds you accountable to yourself.

One of the biggest failings in the financial services industry is the failure to understand the basic need for coaching.

The industry is dominated not by coaches (or even advisors) but by commission based salesmen. They push product as the answer and then go looking for the question. Objectivity is lost, and the client pays the price.

A good wealth coach services his clients with a holistic approach and commits himself to putting the needs of the client first.

Over 10 years, we have refined our process to offer such a service. It's a four-step process called The Wealth Coaching Program.

Step One: The Consultation--We begin every first meeting with a simple question: "What will make this a great meeting for you today?" We want the client to set the agenda. More importantly, we want to know what keeps them up at night.

If on a scale of one to ten (ten means you sleep like Bill Gates, and one means you don't sleep at all), how do you rate your financial situation? If you are a nine or a ten, you are done. Give this book to a friend, and go live your life. No need for any coaching. You are Tiger Woods in 2000 or Michael Jordan during his reign of dominance. You don't need my help.

But if you are more like a seven (or lower), then what has to occur for you to be at a ten, aside from winning the lottery?

We find that it's rarely about the amount of money one has. The most anxious people we've ever met had significant wealth.

Despite that, they were fearful, frustrated, and even angry. To get most people to a ten, it takes a strategy that they have had a hand in designing. They require a plan that details fully the pros and cons, and is simple enough that they can explain it to a friend. Understanding and "buying in" to the plan is just as important as the plan itself. Why? Because if you "buy in" you will probably stick with the plan during those difficult emotional times.

Do you need to be a financial expert to be a ten? No. Just like we don't need to know how a hybrid engine works to drive a car. We do need to know how to start the car (which if you haven't bought a car lately, isn't as easy as it used to be with new push button starts, etc.).

We need to know how to put the car in gear, and how to turn the wheel. We need to know when gas is needed, when to rotate the tires, and when to change the oil. Simple stuff, but it is required.

A well-designed financial strategy answers questions like:

1. How much can I spend during retirement without a strong chance of going broke?

2. What rate of return do I really need on my money, and how can I get it with the least amount of volatility?

3. How can I protect myself from speculation (stock picking, market timing, and track record investing)?

4. How will I deal with catastrophe, such as failing health?

5. How can I legally pay the IRS less?

6. How can I most efficiently transfer my assets at death?

Step Two: The Creation-- Then questions to step one are answered by making you a part of the plan's design.

A good coach listens to what you want to accomplish (I want $X a month for life, after tax, indexed for inflation) and then offers the pros and cons of achieving that goal. And trust me…there are always cons. You need to know them.

Together we draw up the plan. How much of your income do you want guaranteed? Before you say "all of it," know that guaranteed usually comes with two costs: low return and less for your heirs.

If you choose to have some or all of your money in a non-guaranteed portfolio, do you fully understand the likely range of returns? What is your worst year likely to be (statistically)?

And when it happens (and it will), what will you do?

How much (if any) would you like to leave to your children?

How do you wish to handle the cost of custodial care should you need it (and you probably will)?

If you choose to make no changes, what are your chances for success? Are you okay with that?

Step Three: The Consideration--Only after the design is fully complete can the plan be written. Back when Dan's blood results showed he had too much sugar in his blood, he and his doctor together discussed the ups and downs of the strategy: costs, time, denial of certain foods, etc. Once that was outlined, only then did they actually create a written plan.

Medications can be used to fight illness. The doctor doesn't care where you fill the prescription. He simply wants you to fully take the meds.

In personal finance, products are the medication. While a coach can assist you in acquiring them, it should not be a requirement for being coached.

Sadly, we too often see financial advisors offer "free" planning. There is no such thing as free. You will pay for it, one way or another.

Typically, the "plan" is nothing more than a sales proposal to buy a product.

"We'll give you a free plan that will recommend you buy a commission-based product from us."

In addition to delivering the written plan, we provide the client with a list of recommendations on a single page. With each recommendation, we ask a few simple questions:

1. Do you fully understand this recommendation? Do you know the pros and cons?
2. Are you going to implement it (yes or no...never a "let me think about it")?
3. How are you going to implement it? Are you going work with someone (insurance agent, investment advisor)?

No loose ends.

Step Four: The Coaching & Education Stage-- Our firm educates our clients in groups, but coaches them one on one.

Some of the education classes many times reiterate important concepts that are helpful in understanding the long-term issues facing retirement. Other classes delve deeper into the client's emotions. Almost all of our decisions are emotionally based. We need to accept and understand that. By being in tune with our values, we are much more likely to reach a true purpose for our money that reflects these values.

MY OFFER TO YOU

Although not nearly as complicated as many make it out to be, personal finance does have enough complexity that it can only lead some to make mistakes, but also scare others to the point where they do very little in retirement out of fear they will go broke before they die. Lack of taking action will never fix these fears, however.

Few things are more tragic than being filled with regret on one's deathbed, especially if those regrets were avoidable.

For many, it's a matter of getting the right amount of help or just a little coaching. Let us help you.

If you do plan on working with a professional, we've outlined below some suggestions:

1. Begin the relationship with a written plan. Work only with someone who charges you for it. People who give away

advice for free have an ulterior motive, and it's not to offer you objective advice.

2. Ask the potential advisor to explain his worldview on investments. Does he believe that markets are predictable or not? Do they believe in active or passive management? Be sure that his opinion matches what you believe.

3. Credentials do matter. As a recent commercial demonstrated, anyone can call himself or herself a financial advisor. We suggest working with one who has a background and the degrees to prove it.

4. Check to see if FINRA or the SEC has ever reprimanded him or her.

5. Go with your gut. My poor wife could never logically explain to her parents why she married me. Thirteen years later, I think she is happy. She still has to put up with me. I think she went with her gut. It's a feeling. If your gut says "no", then keep looking.

I would love to help you to understand how you can rescue your 401K for your ideal retirement. Since you are reading this book, I am going to offer you a complimentary portfolio MRI.

With this, I will fully analyze your current portfolio and then we will sit down together and go through every piece one on one. We will remove the emotion and simply look at the numbers. We will only then have a path ahead of us using academic principles and Nobel Prize winning research.

You need someone to help you rescue your 401K and retirement from the ticking tax time bomb! I can help! We can also help you plan to be a part of the 0% tax bracket in retirement. Reach out to us!!

APPENDICES

APPENDIX I

THE ROTH 401(K)

Under a regular 401(k), 403(b), or 457(b) governmental plan, a participant chooses to defer a portion of his or her compensation into the plan. Such "elective deferrals" are made on a pre-tax basis, any account growth is tax- deferred, and withdrawals are taxed as ordinary income.[1]

In a qualified Roth contribution program, a participant can choose to have all or part of his or her elective deferrals made to a separate, designated Roth account. Such "designated Roth contributions" are made on an after-tax basis. Growth in the

designated Roth account is tax-deferred and qualified distributions are excluded from gross income.

Other point

---

[1] The discussion here concerns federal income tax law. State or local income tax law maydiffer.

- Separate accounting and recordkeeping are required for the deferrals under the regular, pre-tax portions of a plan and for those made to the after-tax, designated Roth account.

- Individuals whose adjusted gross income exceeds certain limits may not contribute to a regular Roth IRA. There are no such income limits applicable to a designated Roth account.

- For 401(k) plans, contributions to a designated Roth account are elective deferrals for purposes of the Actual Deferral Percentage (ADP) test.

CONTRIBUTIONS

A number of rules apply to contributions to a qualified Roth contribution program:

- **Dollar limitation:** For 2020, a maximum of $19,500 may be contributed. Those who are age 50 and older may make additional contributions of $6,500. A participant may choose to place all of his or her contributions in the regular, pre-tax portion of a plan, all in the designated Roth account, or split the deferrals between the two.

- Employer contributions: Employer contributions will be credited only to the regular, pre-tax portion of a plan they may not be designated as Roth contributions.

- Excess contributions: Excess deferrals to a designated Roth account must be distributed to the participant no later than April 15 of the year following the year in which the excess deferral was made. Otherwise, the excess deferral will be taxed twice, once in the year of deferral and a second time the year a corrective distribution is made.

DISTRIBUTIONS

A distribution from a designated Roth account will be excluded from income if it is made at least five years after a contribution to such an account was first made and at least one of the following applies:

- The participant reaches age 59½;

- The participant dies;

- The participant becomes disabled.

Such distributions are known as "qualified" distributions.

Other points

Nonqualified distributions: If a distribution does not meet the above requirements, it is termed a "nonqualified" distribution. Such distributions are subject to federal income tax, including a 10% premature distribution penalty if the participant is under age 59½ in the year the funds are distributed. Such distributions are taxed under the annuity rules of IRC Sec. 72; any part of a distribution that is attributable to earnings is includable in income; any portion attributable to the original investment (basis) is recovered tax-free. This contrasts sharply with the taxation of nonqualified distributions from a regular Roth IRA account. Nonqualified distributions from a regular Roth IRA are taxed following pre-defined ordering rules under which basis is recovered first, followed by earnings.

- **First-time homebuyer expenses:** In a regular Roth IRA, a qualified distribution may be made to pay for first-time homebuyer expenses. This provision does not apply to distributions from a designated Roth account.

- **Rollovers to designated Roth accounts:** Distributions from the regular, pre-tax portion of a qualified plan may be rolled-over into a designated Roth account. The individual (either the participant or a surviving spouse) must include the distribution in gross income (subject to basis recovery) in the same manner as if the distribution from the pre-tax plan had been rolled over into a Roth IRA.

- **Rollovers from designated Roth accounts:** A distribution from a designated Roth account may only be rolled over into a Roth IRA or another designated Roth account. Such a rollover is not a taxable event

- **Required minimum distributions:** Generally, amounts in a designated Roth account are subject to the required minimum distribution rules applicable to plan participants when they reach age 72. However, a participant can avoid the mandated distributions by rolling over amounts in the designated Roth account into a regular Roth IRA.

WHICH ACCOUNT TO CHOOSE?

The decision as to which type of account should be used will generally be made on factors such as the length of time until retirement (or until the funds are needed), the amount of money available to contribute each year, the participant's current tax situation, and the anticipated marginal tax rate in retirement. An important issue to keep in mind is the overall, lifetime tax burden.

- **Regular 401(k), 403(b), or 457(b) governmental plan:** Generally, individuals with a relatively short period of time until retirement, or who expect that their marginal tax rate will be lower in retirement, will benefit more from a regular, pre-tax qualified retirement plan.
- **Designated Roth account:** Younger individuals with more years until retirement and those who anticipate that their

marginal tax rate will rise in retirement will generally benefit more from a designated Roth account. The fact that contributions to a designated Roth account are after-tax may cause current cash-flow problems for some individuals. Higher income participants may find that taxable income will be higher with a designated Roth account than with a regular pre-tax plan, potentially reducing tax breaks such as the child tax credit or AMT exemption.

- **Both:** Some individuals may choose to contribute to both types of plan, to provide flexibility in retirement.

SEEK PROFESSIONAL GUIDANCE

Because of the complexities involved, the guidance of tax andfinancial professionals is strongly recommended.

APPENDIX II

ROTH IRAs

The Roth IRA differs from the traditional IRA in that contributions are never deductible and, if certain requirements are met, account distributions are free of federal income tax.1

FUNDING A ROTH IRA

Annual contributions: A Roth IRA may be established and funded at any time between January 1 of the current year, up to and including the date an individual's federal income tax return is due, (generally April 15 of the following year), not including extensions.

CONVERSION OF A TRADITIONAL IRA ACCOUNT

A traditional IRA may be converted to a Roth IRA, with the conversion being a taxable event. For the year of conversion the taxpayer must include in gross income previously deducted contributions plus net earnings (or minus net losses). For individual retirement annuities, gross income is generally increased by the fair market value of the contract on the date of conversion (through a redesignation) or distribution (if held inside an IRA). If a retirement annuity is completely surrendered, the cash received is the amount includable in income. Any 10% penalty tax for early withdrawal is waived. However, if a taxpayer withdraws amounts from the Roth IRA within five years of the conversion, the 10% penalty tax will apply to those amounts deemed to be part of the conversion, unless an exception applies.

Prior to 2018, a taxpayer who converted a traditional IRA to a Roth IRA could "undo" the transaction and "recharacterize" the converted funds, moving them back into a traditional IRA.

However, for tax years beginning in 2018, the Tax Cuts and Jobs Act of 2017 (TCJA), permanently repealed the ability to recharacterize a Roth conversion back to a traditional IRA.

TCJA did not repeal the ability of a taxpayer to convert a Roth IRA to a traditional IRA and then recharacterize the converted funds, moving them back into a Roth IRA

ROLLOVERS FROM A QUALIFIED PLAN

Distributions from qualified retirement plans, IRC Sec. 457(b) governmental plans, and IRC Sec. 403(b) plans may also be rolled over to a Roth IRA. These conversions are taxable events, with gross income for the year of conversion being increased by previously deducted contributions plus net earnings (or minus net losses).

Direct rollover from a designated Roth Account: Funds may be rolled into a regular Roth IRA from a designated Roth account that is part of a 401(k), 403(b), or 457(b) governmental plan. Such a rollover is not a taxable event and the filing status and MAGI limitations normally applicable to regular Roth contributions do not apply.

MILITARY DEATH PAYMENTS

Under the provisions of the Heroes Earnings Assistance and Relief Tax Act of 2008, an individual who receives a military death gratuity and/or a payment under the Servicemembers' Group Life Insurance (SGLI) program may contribute to a Roth IRA an amount no greater than the sum of any military death gratuity and SGLI payment. Such a contribution is considered a qualified rollover contribution and must be made within one year of receiving the death gratuity or insurance payment. The annual dollar contribution

limit and income-based phase-out of the dollar contribution limit do not apply to such contributions.

TYPE OF ARRANGEMENTS PERMITTED

There are currently two types of Roth IRAs.

- **Individual retirement accounts:** Trusts or custodial accounts with a corporate trustee or custodian.
- **Individual retirement annuities:** Special annuities issued by a life insurance company.

CONTRIBUTION LIMITS

Limits: For 2020, an individual may contribute (but not necessarily deduct) the lesser of $6,000 or 100% of compensation[2] for the year. For a married couple, an additional $5,500 may be contributed on behalf of a lesser earning (or nonworking) spouse, using a spousal account.

A husband and wife may contribute up to a total of $11,000, as long as their combined compensation is at least that amount.[3]

If an IRA owner is age 50 or older, he or she may contribute an additional $1,000 ($2,000 if the spouse is also age 50 or older).

Other IRAs: The contribution limits for a Roth IRA are coordinated with those of a traditional IRA; a taxpayer may not contribute more than the annual limit for that tax year into a single IRA or a combination of traditional and Roth IRAs. Excess contributions to a traditional or Roth IRA are subject to a 6% excise tax.

---

[2] "Compensation" includes taxable wages, salaries, or commissions or the net income from self-employment

[3] These amounts apply to 2018. For 2017, the maximum allowable contribution was also $5,500 for a single individual and $11,000 for a married couple.

Contribution phase out: For 2020, the maximum contribution to a Roth IRA is phased out for single taxpayers with MAGI between

$124,300 and $139,000. For married couples filing jointly, the phase- out range is a MAGI of $196,000 to $206,000. For married individuals filing separately, the phase-out range is a MAGI of $0 to $10,000.[4]

TAXATION OF DISTRIBUTIONS

A distribution from a Roth IRA that is a "qualified" distribution is excluded from gross income and is not subject to federal income tax. A distribution is qualified if it is made after a five-year waiting period[5] and at least one of the following requirements is met:

- after the taxpayer reaches age 59½; or

---

[4] For 2017, the phase-out ranges were: (1) MFJ – MAGI of $186,000 - $196,000 and (2) Single - $118,000 - $133,000. For those using the MFS filing status, the phase-out range is $0 - $10,000, which does not change.

[5] Generally, five years after a contribution is first made, or amounts are converted to a Roth IRA.

- due to the taxpayer's death; or

- because the taxpayer becomes disabled; or

- to pay for first-time-home-buyer expenses up to $10,000.

The earnings portion of a "non-qualified" distribution is subject to tax. To determine any taxable distribution, the funds are considered to be withdrawn in a specified order

- Any withdrawal is considered to come first from non-deductible contributions, which are not subject to tax.

- After all contributions have been withdrawn, any conversion amounts are considered next. A distribution of converted funds is not included in gross income, but may be subject to the 10% premature distribution penalty if the funds are withdrawn within five years of being converted.

- Once all contributions and conversions have been withdrawn, any remaining funds are deemed to be earnings, and, when distributed, are included in gross income.

PREMATURE DISTRIBUTIONS

If a taxable distribution is received prior to age 59½, a 10% penalty tax is added to the regular income tax due, unless one or more of the following exceptions apply:

- A distribution is made because of the death or disability of the account owner.

- A withdrawal is part of a scheduled series of substantially equal periodic payments.

- A distribution is rolled-over into another Roth IRA.

- A withdrawal is used to pay for deductible medical expenses

- The distribution is used to pay for certain qualified higher- education expenses.

- Amounts are withdrawn to pay for first-time homebuyer expenses of up to $10,000.

- In certain situations, to pay health insurance premiums for unemployed individuals.

- Distributions by certain military reservists called to active duty after 09/11/2001.

- A distribution is transferred to a Health Savings Account (HSA).

- In case of an IRS levy on the account.

OTHER DIFFERENCES

There are several other significant differences between the traditional and Roth IRAs:

Contributions after age 72: Contributions to a Roth IRA may be made even after the taxpayer has reached age 70½, as long as the taxpayer has compensation at least equal to the contribution, subject to the phase-out rules.

Distribution requirements: Roth IRAs are not subject to the mandatory required minimum distribution (RMD) rules during the life of the owner (triggered at age 72) applicable to traditional IRAs. However, there are post-death minimum distribution rules applicable to non-spousal beneficiaries who inherit a Roth account

CHARITABLE DISTRIBUTIONS

Federal income tax law provides for an exclusion from gross income of up to $100,000 for distributions made from a Roth or traditional IRA directly to a qualified charitable organization. Such a distribution counts towards the taxpayer's RMD requirements.

The IRA owner (Or beneficiary of an inherited IRA) must be at least age 70½ when the distribution is made. No charitable deduction is allowed for such a qualified charitable distribution.

TRANSFERS TO HEALTH SAVINGS ACCOUNTS (HSAs)

Federal law allows for a limited, one-time, direct transfer of funds from an IRA to an HSA. If certain requirements are met, any otherwise taxable portion of the distribution is excluded from income and the 10% early distribution penalty will not apply.

INVESTMENT ALTERNATIVES

- **Banks, savings and loans, credit unions:** Certificates of deposit in Roth IRAs are generally insured by either the FDIC or the NCUA for amounts up to $250,000. Fixed and variable rates are available. There may be stiff penalties for early withdrawal.

- **Annuities:** Traditional, fixed individual retirement annuities issued by life insurance companies can guarantee fixe monthly income at retirement and may include a disability- waiver-of-premium provision. Variable annuities do not guarantee a fixed monthly income at retirement.

- **Money market:** Yield fluctuates with the economy. Investor cannot lock in higher interest rates. It is easy to switch to other investments.

- **Mutual funds:** A wide variety of mutual funds with many investment objectives are available.

- **Zero coupon bonds:** Bonds are issued at a deep discount from face value. There are no worries about reinvesting interest payments. Zero coupon bonds are subject to inflation risk and interest rate risk.

- **Stocks:** A wide variety of investments (and risk) is possible. Losses are generally not deductible.

- **Limited partnerships:** Some limited partnerships are especially designed for qualified plans, specifically in the areas of real estate and mortgage pools.

- **Prohibited Investments or Transactions**

- **Life insurance:** Roth IRAs cannot include life insurance contracts.

- **Loans to IRA taxpayer:** Self-borrowing triggers a constructive distribution of the entire amount in an IRA.

- **Collectibles:** Purchase of art works, antiques, metals, gems, stamps, etc., will be treated as a taxable distribution. Coins issued under state law and certain U.S. gold, silver and platinum coins are exceptions. Certain kinds of bullion may be purchased.

OTHER FACTORS TO CONSIDER

- What is the yield? More frequent compounding will produce a higher return. Is the interest rate fixed or variable? If interest rates drop, a fixed rate may be better, especially if you can make future contributions at the same fixed rate. If interest rates go up, you may be able to roll the account to another Roth IRA.

- How often can you change investments? Is there a charge?
- Refunds of federal income taxes may be directly deposited into an IRA.
- Federal bankruptcy law protects assets in Roth IRA accounts, up to $1,283,025.[6] Funds rolled over from qualified plans are protected without limit.

---

[6] Effective April 1, 2016. The limit is indexed for inflation every three years.

APPENDIX III

ROTH IRA CONVERSION FACTORS TO CONSIDER

Before 2010, taxpayers[7] with a modified adjusted gross income (MAGI)[8] in excess of $100,000, or who filed their federal income tax returns using the Married Filing Separately filing status, were prohibited from converting a traditional IRA to a Roth IRA. Beginning in 2010, however, these prohibitions no longer applied.

For many individuals, the ability to convert a traditional IRA to a Roth IRA represents a significant tax planning opportunity.[9]

---

[7] The discussion here concerns federal income tax law. State or local law may differ.

[8] Modified adjusted gross income (MAGI) is a taxpayer's adjusted gross income (AGI) with certain deductions or exclusions added back. For most taxpayers, MAGI and AGI are the same.

[9] Although the discussion here focuses on traditional IRAs, the same rules apply to amounts converted from a SEP IRA or SIMPLE IRA to a Roth IRA. Funds in a SIMPLE IRA that do not meet the two-year period described in IRC Sec. 72(t)(6) may not be converted. Distributions from

PAY ME LATER OR PAY ME NOW

With a traditional IRA, and assuming certain requirements are met, contributions are deductible in the year they are made. The tax due on the contributions, and the tax due on any earnings or growth, is deferred until funds are distributed from the account, typically at retirement. From an income tax perspective, this is a "pay me later" scenario.

With a Roth IRA, contributions are never deductible; they are made with funds that have already been taxed. If certain requirements are met, both the contributions and any earnings or growth are received income-tax free when withdrawn from the account. From an income tax perspective, this is a "pay me now" scenario.

A taxpayer who elects to convert a traditional IRA to a Roth IRA has chosen to pay the income tax now rather than waiting until the future to pay it. To justify a conversion, the benefit of

---

IRC Sec. 401(a) qualified retirement plans, IRC Sec. 457(b) governmental plans, and IRC Sec. 403(b) plans may also be rolled over into a Roth IRA

not paying taxes tomorrow should be greater than the cost of paying taxes today

BENEFITS OF ROTH IRAS

The benefits of holding assets in a Roth IRA can be considerable:

- **During life – tax-free income:** Assuming that certain requirements are met, including a five-taxable year waiting period after a contribution is first made to a Roth IRA for the owner, "qualified" distributions are received income-tax free.

- **At death – income-tax free to beneficiaries:** At death, the value of the Roth IRA is includable in the account owner's estate, subject to federal estate tax. A surviving spouse can treat an inherited Roth IRA as his or her own, with the proceeds being received income-tax free, and with no required minimum distributions. For non- spousal beneficiaries, and assuming that the five-year waiting period requirement has been met, the proceeds are received income-tax free. After the owner's death, however, non-spousal beneficiaries must take certain required minimum distributions.

- **No lifetime required minimum distributions:** Federal income tax law mandates that certain required minimum distributions be made from traditional IRAs, beginning when the account owner reaches age 72. For Roth IRAs, there are no minimum distribution requirements during the lifetime of the account owner.

- **No age limit on contributions:** As long as a taxpayer has "compensation" (such as wages or self-employment income), contributions may be made to a Roth IRA regardless of the taxpayer's age, subject to the modified adjusted gross income limitations.

THE COST OF CONVERSION

Converting a traditional IRA to a Roth IRA is a currently taxable event. For the year the converted assets are distributed, the taxpayer must include in gross income all previously deducted contributions, plus net earnings (or minus net losses). For individual retirement annuities, gross income is generally increased by the fair market value of the contract on the date of conversion (through a re-designation) or distribution (if held inside an IRA). If a retirement annuity is completely surrendered, the cash received is the amount includable in income. Any 10% penalty tax for early withdrawal is waived.

If a taxpayer has traditional IRA accounts that hold both deductible and non-deductible amounts, he or she may not "cherry- pick" and convert only the non-deductible contributions.[10] Instead, the value of all IRA accounts is added together and a ratio is calculated to determine the tax-free portion of any conversion.[11]

Example: Paul has a traditional IRA to which he has made

$20,000 in non-deductible contributions. This year, when he converts the account to a Roth IRA, the balance in this IRA is

---

[10] Because they have already been taxed, non-deductible contributions are generally not taxable when converted from a traditional IRA to a Roth IRA.

[11] If all of the contributions to the traditional IRA were deductible, a taxpayer may elect to roll over everything, or pick and choose which accounts or portions of an account to convert.

$30,000. Paul also has a separate IRA containing $70,000 in pre-tax contributions rolled over from a 401(k) plan with a previous employer. The total value of both accounts is $100,000. His "non-deductible" ratio is thus 20%, ($20,000 ÷ $100,000). When Paul converts the $30,000 in his non-deductible IRA, he may exclude only $6,000 (20% x $30,000) from gross income. The remaining $24,000 ($30,000 - $6,000) is includable in his gross income, subject to tax.

SITUATIONS FAVORING CONVERSION TO A ROTH IRA

- **Small account values:** If the dollar amount in the traditional IRA is small, the income- tax cost to convert today would be relatively low.
- **Longer time to retirement:** A longer period of time until retirement allows for greater future growth, necessary to recoup the up-front cost of paying the tax now.
- **Cash to pay the taxes:** Where will the money come from to pay the extra taxes? It's usually better if the account owner has sufficient cash outside of the IRA to pay the tax. Could

the funds used to pay the tax today provide a greater return if invested elsewhere?

- **IRA income not needed:** Some individuals have adequate retirement income from other sources, so that IRA monies are not needed to fund retirement. During the lifetime of the account owner, a Roth IRA has no minimum distribution requirements.

- **Higher future tax bracket:** If a taxpayer anticipates being in a higher tax bracket in the future, paying the tax today, at lower rates, is a logical step. Being taxed at a higher marginal rate may be the result of legislative changes, having a higher taxable income, or a change in filing status, such as when a couple divorces or a spouse dies.

SITUATIONS NOT FAVORING CONVERSION

In some situations, converting a traditional IRA to a Roth IRA may not be appropriate:

- **Retirement begins soon:** If there is only a short time before retirement begins, there may not be enough time for future growth to offset the cost of paying the tax today.

- **High IRA account values:** If the dollar amount in the traditional IRA is large, the tax bill resulting from the conversion will likely be expensive; the conversion could push a taxpayer into a higher marginal tax bracket or make Social Security benefits taxable

- **No cash to pay the taxes:** A taxpayer may not have the cash outside the IRA to pay the extra tax that results from the conversion. Taking funds from the IRA to pay the increased tax reduces the amount left in the account to grow into the future. If the account owner is under age 59½ at the time these extra funds are withdrawn from the IRA, a 10% penalty on the amount not converted will likely be added to the tax bill.

- **Lower future tax rates:** If a taxpayer anticipates being in a lower tax bracket in the future, paying the tax today, at higher marginal tax rates, makes no sense.

RECHARACTERIZATION

Prior to 2018, a taxpayer who converted a traditional IRA to a Roth IRA could "undo" the transaction and "recharacterize" the converted funds, moving them back into a traditional IRA.

However, for tax years beginning in 2018, the Tax Cuts and Jobs Act of 2017 (TCJA), permanently repealed the ability to recharacterize a Roth conversion back to a traditional IRA.

SEEK PROFESSIONAL GUIDANCE

The decision to convert all or part of a traditional IRA to a Roth IRA is an individual one. A thorough analysis requires careful consideration of a number of income tax, investment, and estat planning factors, over an extended time horizon. The advice and guidance of appropriate financial, tax, and investment professionals is strongly recommended.

APPENDIX IV

IRC SEC. 72(t)(2)(A)(iv)

Generally, taxable distributions from employer-sponsored qualified retirement plans, and from traditional and Roth IRAs, made before the account owner reaches age 59½, are subject to a 10% "early" withdrawal penalty.12 One exception to this 10% penalty is for distributions taken as a series of "substantially equal periodic payments."[12]

This exception applies to distributions made, at least once a year, over the life (or life expectancy) of the participant, or over the joint lives (or joint life expectancies) of the participant and a beneficiary. The payments must continue unchanged (except for death or disability) for the longer of: (a) five years (five years from the date of the first payment), or (b) the participant reaches age

---

[12] The discussion here concerns federal income tax law. State or local law may differ. Under federal law, the 10% penalty generally applies to distributions which are includable in gross income

59½. Otherwise, the 10% penalty will be applied retroactively and interest will be charged

CALCULATING THE SUBSTANTIALLY-EQUAL PERIODIC PAYMENT

In Notice 89-25, 11989-1, CB 662, Q&A-12 (March 20, 1989), the IRS listed three acceptable methods of calculating such a distribution:

- **Required minimum distribution (RMD):** The annual payment is determined using a method acceptable for calculating the required minimum distribution required under IRC Sec. 401(a)(9). In general, the account balance is divided by a life expectancy factor, resulting in a payment which changes from year to year.

- **Fixed amortization method:** Payment under this method is similar to the annual amount required to pay off a loan (equal to the amount in the plan at the start of distributions), at a reasonable interest rate, over the remainder of one's life. The dollar amount of the payment remains the same in each subsequent year.

- **Fixed annuitization:** An annuity factor is determined from a reasonable mortality table at an interest rate which is then reasonable for the age of the recipient of the distribution. The payment is determined for the first distribution and remains the same in each subsequent year.

REVENUE RULING 2002-6

On October 3, 2002, the IRS released Revenue Ruling 2002-62, to address questions raised by taxpayers who had begun to receive distributions under IRC Sec. 72(t)(2)(A)(iv) and who had been adversely affected by a declining stock market. This ruling contained the following key points.

- It expanded the guidance given in Q&A 12 of IRS Notice 89-25 to, among other things, incorporate into the calculation process the new life expectancy tables issued in

April, 2002, with regard to required minimum distributions from IRAs and qualified plans.

- Allowed a participant who had been using either the fixed amortization method or the fixed annuitization method to make a one-time change to the RMD method.

- Specified that if a participant who is using an acceptable method to calculate the required substantially equal periodic payments exhausts the assets in an account prior to the required time period, the "cessation of payments will not be treated as a modification of the series of payments."

The guidance provided in Revenue Ruling 2002-62 replaced the guidance of IRS Notice 89-25 for any series of payments beginning on or after January 1, 2003. If distributions began before 2003 under any method that satisfied IRC Sec. 72(t)(2)(A)(iv), a change to the required minimum distribution calculation method may be made at any time.

COMPARING THE THREE METHODS[13]

Assumptions:

Plan or IRA account balance on 12/31 of the previous year:

$400,000 Age of participant in distribution year: 50 Single life expectancy at age 50: 34.2[14] Interest rate assumed: 2.98%[15] Distribution period: Single life only

Required minimum distribution method: For the current year, the annual distribution amount is calculated by dividing account balance by the participant's life expectancy.

$400,000 / 34.2 = $11,696

Fixed amortization method: Distribution amount is calculated by amortizing the account balance over the number of years of the participant's single life expectancy. The calculation is

---

[13] The examples shown are from the IRS web site, www.irs.gov, "Retirement Plans FAQs Regarding Substantially Equal Periodic Payments," August 4, 2017.

[14] Derived from the Single Life Table found in Reg.1.401(a)(9)-9, Q&A-1. The Uniform Lifetime Table found in Appendix A of Revenue Ruling 2002-62 or the Joint and Last Survivor table of Reg.1.401(a)(9)-9, Q&A-3 may also be used.

[15] This rate is equal to 120% of the federal mid-term rate. In these IRS examples, the rate for April 2011 is used. This value will fluctuate and changes monthly.

the same as in determining the payment required to pay off a loan.

$400,000 x (.0298 / (1 − (1 + .0298)^−34.2)) = $18,811

Fixed annuitization method: The distribution amount is equal to the account balance divided by an annuity factor that for the present value of an annuity of one dollar per year paid over the life of year-old participant. Such annuity factors are typically calculated by an actuary. In this case, the age-50 annuity factor (21.345) is based on the mortality table in Appendix B of Revenue Ruling 2002-62 and an interest rate of 2.98%.

$400,000 / 21.345 = $18,740

Method	Annual Withdrawal
Required minimum distribution	$11,696
Fixed amortization	$18,811
Fixed annuitization	$18,740

APPENDIX V

CASH VALUE LIFE INSURANCE

ACCUMULATING FUNDS TO MEET SAVINGS GOALS

Saving money to reach an accumulation goal is a problem many of us face. Some goals, such as retirement or a college fund for a child, are long-term savings goals. Many of us also have shorter-term savings goals such as a vacation or a Christmas or holiday fund.

Whatever the objective, the basic problem is the same, i.e. where to put money aside to reach a particular savings goal. For many short-term goals, a savings account at a local bank or credit union is a popular choice. For college funding, Coverdell IRAs or IRC Sec. 529 plans are often used. For retirement savings, many individual depend on Individual Retirement Accounts (IRAs) or employer- sponsored retirement plans such as an IRC Sec. 401(k) plan.

An additional option for long-term savings, one that is sometimes overlooked, is using a cash value life insurance policy.

WHAT IS CASH VALUE LIFE INSURANCE?

Life insurance comes in two basic variations, "term" insurance and "cash value" life insurance. Term life insurance can be compared to auto insurance. Protection is provided for a specified period of time or "term." No death benefits are paid unless the insured dies during the term the policy is in force. If the insured lives beyond the term period, the policy generally expires with nothing returned to the policy owner.

In addition to providing a death benefit, "cash value" life insurance also provides for the tax- deferred accumulation of money inside the policy. These funds can be used by the policy owner while the insured is alive to provide the resources for needs such as funding a college education, making improvements to the home, or starting a business. When the policy owner uses the cash values to meet such needs, he or she is said to have used the "living benefits" of a cash value life insurance policy.

WHEN TO CONSIDER CASH VALUE LIFE INSURANCE

Using a cash value life insurance policy to reach a saving goal works best in certain situations:

- **A need for life insurance death benefit** apart from the need for additional savings, an individual should have a need for the death benefit that life insurance provides. For example, such a need exists when an individual has a dependent spouse or children who would suffer economically if the individual died. Someone with a large estate might need additional cash at death to pay estate and other taxes as well as final expenses.

- **Other savings aren't enough:** Because of limitations in federal tax law,[16] other accumulation vehicles might not

---

[16] The discussion here concerns federal income tax law. State or local tax law may vary widely.

allow enough money to be put aside to meet a particular savings goal.

- **Time frame:** Ideally, there should be at least 10 to 15 years between today and the time the money will be needed. Because of mortality expenses and other policy charges, significant cash value accumulations are generally deferred until a policy has been in force for a number of years. Additionally, federal income tax law affects the design of cash value life insurance policies as well as the taxation of cash value withdrawals in the early years a policy is in force

- **Insurable:** The insured needs to be healthy enough to have a policy issued on his or her life.

- **An ongoing obligation:** Cash value life insurance policies tend to have a higher premium cost than comparable term life policies. Paying the premiums over a number of years represents an ongoing financial obligation, to both keep the policy in force and achieve the savings goal.

INCOME TAX CONSIDERATIONS

There are a number of income tax issues to keep in mind when considering any life insurance policy. The death benefit payable under a life insurance contract because of the death of the insured is generally received income-tax free. Federal income taxation of life insurance "living benefits" is more complicated:

- **Tax-deferred growth:** The growth of cash value inside a life insurance policy is tax- deferred.

- **Cost recovery rule:** Amounts withdrawn from a cash-value life insurance contract are included in gross income (and become subject to tax) only when they exceed the policy owner's basis in the policy. This basis is also known as the "investment in the contract." This effectively treats withdrawals from the policy first as a non-taxable return of premium and secondly as taxable income.

- **Investment in the contract:** The total of all premium paid less any policy dividends and any other prior tax-free distributions received.

- **Policy dividends:** Some "participating" life policies pay what are termed "dividends." Such dividends are a return of a portion of the policy owner's previously paid premiums. Policy dividends are not taxable until they exceed the owner's basis in the life insurance contract.

- **Policy loans:** Some cash value life insurance policies allow the policy owner to borrow at interest a portion of the accumulated cash value. While a policy is in force, policy loans are generally not taxable. However, if a policy is surrendered with a loan outstanding, taxable income will result to the extent that the unpaid loan amount exceeds the owner's basis in the contract.

- **Modified Endowment Contracts (MECs):** Some life insurance policies – primarily because there are large premium payments in the early years of the contract – are termed "Modified Endowment Contracts," or MECs. Under federal income tax law, distributions from a policy considered to be a MEC are treated differently than distributions from non- MEC policies. Withdrawals from a MEC (including a policy loan) will first be taxed as current income until all of the policy earnings have been taxed. If the owner is under age 59½, a 10% penalty also applies, unless the payments are due to disability or are annuity type payments. Once all policy earnings have been distributed (and taxed), any further withdrawals are treated as a non-taxable return of premium.

ACCESSING THE CONTRACT'S CASH VALUES

When the time comes to use the accumulated cash values, withdrawals from the policy should be done in such a way as to avoid current income taxation (to the extent possible) and keep the policy in force.

- **Withdrawal to basis:** Initially a policy owner can take withdrawals (partial policy surrenders) until he or she has withdrawn an amount equal to the basis in the policy.

- **Switching to policy loans:** Once the basis has been withdrawn, the policy owner then begins using non-taxable policy loans. The interest payable on these policy loans is typically much less than a loan from a commercial bank or credit union.

- **A combination:** A policy owner can also use a combination of withdrawals and policy loans.

- Caveats: There are a number of issues that a policy owner needs to keep in mind:

- Withdrawals reduce the death benefit available under the policy

- If an insured dies with a policy loan outstanding, the policy's death benefit is reduced by the amount of the loan balance.

- Excessive use of withdrawals and policy loans can result in the policy lapsing. Such a lapse can result in unexpected, negative tax results as well as the loss of a valuable financial asset.

A MULTI-FUNCTION TOOL

Used appropriately, cash value life insurance can serve as financial tool with multiple uses. It can be used, in conjunction with more traditional savings vehicles, as a way to accumulate funds for long- term savings goals. At the same time the policy can, if the insured dies, provide a death benefit when the funds are most needed.

SEEK PROFESSIONAL GUIDANCE

Determining the appropriate amount of life insurance, the best type of policy to meet the needs of an individual's specific situation, and planning when and how to access a policy's cash values can be complex and confusing. The advice and guidance of trained insurance, tax, and other financial professionals is strongly recommended.

APPENDIX VI

LIFE INSURANCE– LTC COMBINATION POLICIES

Providing for health care is a key part of retirement planning. For most Americans age 65 and over, the federal government's Medicare program, and its various components, provides most of the resources to take care of a typical retiree's health care needs.

One health care need that is only minimally covered by Medicare is that of long-term care (LTC). LTC is the term used to describe a variety of maintenance or "custodial" services required by individuals who are chronically disabled, ill, or infirm. Depending on individual needs, LTC may include nursing home care, assisted living, home health care, or adult day care.

Not everyone will need LTC in retirement. For those that do, LTC is expensive. In 2017, for example, the national median cost for a resident in an assisted living facility was $45,000 per year; the national median cost for a semi-private nursing home room was $85,755 per year.[17] The problem, then, is how to pay for an expensive need that may, or may not, occur.

One answer has been that of a stand-alone, long-term care insurance policy. Should the need arise, a LTC policy can furnish some or all of the resources needed to pay for care. LTC insurance can be expensive, however, and most policies allow for the possibility of future rate increases. Plus, if an individual uses few (or none) of a policy's benefits, there is a sense that the money was not well spent.

One alternative to a traditional LTC insurance policy is that of a "combination" policy that links a cash-value life insurance policy with a tax-qualified, long-term care benefit. These combination policies take advantage of federal[18] income tax law which allows for payment of "accelerated death benefits," up to the policy's death benefit, should the insured need long- term care. If LTC services are required, the policy death benefit can be used to help pay these costs. If LTC services are not needed, or

---

[17] Source: The Genworth 2017 Cost of Care Summary, page 2.

[18] The discussion here concerns federal income tax law. State of local income tax law may differ.

only a portion of the death benefit is used to pay LTC expenses, any remaining policy death benefit (less any policy loans) passes to beneficiaries named by the insured. Such a combination policy is most appropriate when there is a need for both life insurance and long-term care protection.

- **Long-term care "riders":** In return for paying an additional premium, a "rider" can be added to a life insurance policy which allows the insurance carrier to advance the policy's death benefit to the insured, if long-term care is required. With some policies, a second rider can be added to increase the total dollar amount available to pay for LTC services, beyond the policy's original death benefit.

- **Benefit "triggers":** Under federal law, tax-free, accelerated death benefits can be paid from the policy when the insured is considered to be either "terminally ill" (death is expected within 24 months) or "chronically ill." For long-term care purposes,[19] an insured is considered to be chronically ill when he or she is either (1) expected to be

---

[19] See IRC. Sec. 7702(b).

unable to perform for 90 days two of six activities of daily living (eating, toileting, transferring, bathing, dressing, and maintaining continence), or (2) suffers from a cognitive impairment such as Alzheimer's, dementia, or Parkinson's disease. With some policies, a more restrictive definition requires the underlying chronic condition to be permanent.

- **Elimination period:** Once the insured is determined to qualify, long-term care payments can begin after a waiting, or "elimination" period, which can range from 60- 100 days. The elimination period usually only has to be satisfied one time.

- **Monthly LTC benefit amount:** The monthly LTC benefit is a set percentage of the total death benefit, typically selected by the policy owner when the policy is purchased. The table below shows the payment amount and length of time for a hypothetical policy with a $100,000 death benefit:

Payout Percentage	Exemption Amount	Payout Length

1%	$1,000 per month	100 months
2%	$2,000 per month	50 months
3%	$3,000 per month	33 months
4%	$4,000 per month	25 months
5%	$5,000 per month	20 months

- **Effect of LTC payments on policy death benefit:** As LTC benefits are paid out, the policy's death benefit is reduced dollar-for-dollar.

- **Indemnity vs. actual expenses:** Some policies pay benefits on an indemnity or cash basis, meaning that once payments begin the monthly payment is the same regardless of the dollar amount of LTC expenses incurred. Policies that pay benefits on an expense basis pay the lesser of the monthly benefit or the actual LTC expenses incurred. If LTC expenses are less than the normal monthly payment, any unused balance is held over, potentially extending the benefit period.

- **Paying for the policy:** In many cases, a life insurance policy with LTC benefits is funded with a large, single premium. A few policies are paid through periodic premium payments. If appropriate, an existing cash-value life insurance may be exchanged tax- free for a new combination policy.

- **Underwriting:** Some policies, typically those funded with a large, single premium, use a streamlined, simplified underwriting process, with no medical exam. Other policies may require a medical exam and a complete health history.

- **Taxability of benefits:** Depending on the type of policy, long-term care benefits are received income-tax free under either IRC Sec. 101(g) or IRC Sec. 7702B.

- **Rate guarantees:** With many life insurance policies, because the death benefit is a pre- defined amount, the premiums are often guaranteed not to change. With a few types of life insurance, the premium rates may increase under certain conditions, but normally within a specified range.

- **Guaranteed return of premium:** Certain single-premium policies provide for a return of the premium paid (within a specified period of time) if the insured decides not to keep the policy. Life insurance policies which are paid for through periodic payments typically do not have this feature

- **Residual death benefit:** In some instance, a policy may include a "residual" death benefit. If this feature is included, even though the policy's death benefits are exhausted through LTC benefit payments, the policy will still pay a small amount (typically 5% - 10% of the initial death benefit) at the insured's death. This benefit allows the survivors to pay for funeral and other final expenses.

OTHER FACTORS TO CONSIDER

There are a number of other factors to keep in mind when considering a life insurance-LTC combination policy:

- **Not considered state "partnership" LTC policies:** Life-insurance-LTC combination policies generally do not qualify as state "partnership" LTC policies. An insured individual with a partnership LTC policy can keep a much larger dollar amount of assets, while still qualifying for

Medicaid, once the partnership LTC policy benefits are exhausted. Normally, an individual must be nearly destitute before Medicaid will pay for long-term care.

- **Effect of inflation:** Over time, the cost of LTC, like many other things that we buy, will increase. Since it may be many years in the future before long-term care is needed, consider a combination policy that offers a cost-of-living (COLI) rider. Without such a rider, there is a risk that a policy's LTC benefits will not keep up with increases in the cost of long-term care. Generally, once a policy is in force, the death benefit does not increase. Certain types of policies (variable life, variable universal life) have a death benefit that may increase, depending on investment results.

- **Most funded with a large, single premium:** Most life insurance-LTC combination policies are funded with a large, single premium payment. In many instances, a minimum of $25,000 - $75,000 is required to purchase a significant LTC benefit amount.

- **Is this the right tool?** A combination life insurance- LTC combination may not be the right tool if, for example, the insured is already covered by adequate life insurance. If there is a potential need for additional retirement income, a deferred annuity-LTC combination may be a better fit. For some individuals, a stand-alone LTC policy is more appropriate.

SEEK PROFESSIONAL GUIDANCE

One key part of a well-prepared retirement plan is looking ahead to the possible need for long-term care. The advice and guidance of trained financial and insurance professionals, in sorting out the various options for meeting this need, is strongly recommended.

ABOUT THE AUTHOR

Ryan J. Fleming "The Pilot's Advisor"
President & Founder
MBA, Series 7, Series 66

Ryan J. Fleming is President and Founder of the Fleming Financial Group, LLC, a Registered Investment Advisory firm that caters specifically to profession pilots.

Mr. Fleming is a 2001 graduate of the United States Air Force Academy, where he majored in Business Management and played intercollegiate football. After graduation, Mr. Fleming served as an Acquisition and Procurement Officer in the United States Air

Force. He negotiated, managed, and administered large multi-million-dollar government contracts in the Special Operations world.

In 2004, he earned his MBA from the University of Arkansas with a specialization in Human Resource Management. During the same time, he gained a wealth of knowledge and experience as a real estate investment consultant.

In 2005, he attended flight school, and after receiving his wings as an Air Force Pilot, he served multiple tours of duty in Iraq and Afghanistan where he flew the C-17A in direct support of the War on Terror.

Upon leaving active military service, he entered the financial services industry where he was a Registered Representative for Cantella & Company, a SEC registered Broker/Dealer, located in the financial district of Boston. After building his practice for a few years, Mr. Fleming knew the best thing for his clients and their future was to start his own firm. In 2009, the Fleming Financial Group, LLC was founded.

To learn more about the Fleming Financial Group, LLC

and Ryan's financial coaching services, email him:

ryan@flemingfg.com

Or visit www.flemingfg.com and

www.pilotsadvisor.com

https://www.youtube.com/watch?v=AKBKFHYGBBw

Made in the USA
Monee, IL
24 November 2021

82622378R00075